Candidly Speaking

Suranjali Seal

BookLeaf Publishing

India | USA | UK

Made with ❤ on the BookLeaf Publishing Platform
www.bookleafpub.in
www.bookleafpub.com

Dedication

To my dear parents and my loving husband who taught me what love is.

Preface

Dear Reader,

This book captures my heart and mind in words and stanzas. It is a product of years of dreaming, hoping and trying; Days of planning, observing and creating; Minutes of reflecting, recollecting and thinking; Seconds of loving, giving and feeling. I am an islander heart, with a mountaineer mind, autumn moods and sunset vibes and you will find all of these reflected in this poetry collection. I hope you connect with these little pieces of my heart and find sunlight or a beacon of hope or just simple joy in reading them.

Acknowledgements

I feel that some things come naturally to us by virtue of being human beings and these include the capacity to love, share, support and be kind to one another. So first of all I would like to thank God, for gifting me with a world full of such people that make living life worthwhile. Thank you for gifting me a world to observe and revel in with all its wonders, experiences and lessons without which, poetry would not be possible. I want to thank all the people who have made my world a better place by simply being in it and standing by my side, especially in this endeavor of writing a poetry book which was a long sought after dream for me. I want to thank my parents for their unconditional love, sacrifices and efforts towards my upbringing, that are the main pillars to making me who I am today as a human being.

Thank you Maa and Babaie for leading by example and being my support system. I want to thank my loving husband for being my home and a mentor to me, especially whenever I second guessed myself. His love and support has always brought me back to my focus, my dreams, my aspirations and my inner self. So, dear Abhay, I thank you sincerely for justifying being called the better-half of myself.

It is no doubt a wonderful feeling when family and loved ones bring stars together to make your dreams come true. But, when a friendly whishing star comes along the way, at the right time and offers to help you on your journey and become a part of it, it becomes a blessing to cherish for a lifetime. So, I want to thank BookLeaf Publishing for being my wishing star and providing me a platform through which I could share my thoughts and feelings to the world.

Finally, I would like to thank you, dear Readers, for giving me and my world a chance and choosing to be a part of it.

Wine

I carefully observed Evening today
And was immediately allured to her sunset sky-
All her captivating maneuvers,
Her orange touch and fire eye.

The Wind swayed,
The stars peeped,
As the sky danced in classy calm,
The clouds uncorked the Moon into view,
Pouring out the oldest wonder of Nature -
A fantastic evening!

It was intoxicating -
The desire to submerge in the sky,
Bathing in those crimson hues
And becoming a part of
Earth's bottle of wine.

-Suranjali Seal

Just For Me

Craving for warmth on a grey morning,
I rushed out into the shadowland,
Spotted a pool of sunlight yellow,
Carelessly warming Winter's hand.

I found a place beneath his sleeves,
Casually forgetting the darkened hills,
The Sun enjoyed my friendly respite
And asked Winter to stand still.

I looked around the cold silhouette,
And the spotlight that made way through the leaves,
The Sun that shines for the whole world, I felt,
Was shining that day just for me.

-Suranjali Seal

Colour Of My Peach Tree

They cradled me in a bed of rules,
And told me what I shouldn't do,
Said the creases on my skirt,
Weren't the same ones as a shirt's,
My doll house was used as a tool.

Then there were those in my town
Who fought endlessly for the crown
Of sunshine paving the way
For the world to hear what we have to say -
Footsteps from the ends of time.

The bun on my hair was full of dreams,
But, Blue had coloured me in Pink,
Until that day when I let it loose,
Letting it fly in triumphant hues,
Ignoring what the world would think.

Courage was the colour of my peach tree.
-Suranjali Seal

Love Story

When the Ocean cries,
The shore opens his arms
breathing comfort,
She rushes into his being,
And he calms the tumult in her heart,
Whispering,
"I will always be here for you."

-An eternal love story.

-Suranjali Seal

Autumn

I sit by my window
Watching Autumn rustle by in leaves
That brush against sidewalks and dreams,
Through hot chocolate moods and coffee mugs,
Between folded mufflers and sweater hugs,
Alongside alley cats and furry paws,
Within cookie jars and bookstores,
In little tricks and lots of treats,
Among pumpkin faces and woollen weaves,
Amidst checkered skirts and overcoats
And movie nights and bookish quotes -
Fall permeates through our hearts.

It's like comfort making its way into our daily lives,
Winding down for the next season that is to come,
Embracing changes that teach us to thrive
Aiding the tomorrow we are to become.

The air is cinnamon,
The streets gold,

The sky is vintage
In the weather's hold,
We are all Autumn this season-
red, yellow, orange and bold.

-Suranjali Seal

Envy

The sheets that hug you on starry nights,
The Cup that kisses you every morning,
The Wind that greets your hair
And the flowers that caress your mellow fingers,
Are the subjects of my greatest envy.

-Suranjali Seal

Autumn's Fairytale

Autumn dressed in golden hues,
Knocked on my window pane,
In the form of a leaf rustling by
He presented the memories of Summer
running through his veins -

It was about the night that they danced away
At least that's how the story goes,
Till orange streets graced her retreating steps
As the season's called her home.

Now Autumn sighs through yellow woods,
Reminiscing in verse and pumpkin cheer,
Waiting for Winter to seep into maple leaves,
For then Summer will again be near.

-Suranjali Seal

She Magic

Twirling chiffon,
Pleated perfection,
Celebrated curls,
Highlighted heels.
Panther eyes,
Drunken hips,
Perfumed words,
Sunset lips.
Sunflower gaze,
Voice of moonlight,
Smiling mystery
Angelic sight -

She was Magic tonight.

-Suranjali Seal

Tear

You stood at the edge of my cliff,
Wanting to fall onto concrete,
My soul wrapped your tender heart
And pulled you back to me.
You fall in joy,
You fall in sorrow,
Yours is a careless beauty in some way,
But today you fall for faults not your own,
So Dear Tear,
I am not letting you fall today.

-Suranjali Seal

I am Fire

I - born of fire,
You- for I cannot remember you in any other way-
You, for me, have always been defeated.

This cosmic play in truce with duty
Entwined the six of us together,
And on that day too,
I, was fire,
You- with your unquestionable obedience -
Was defeated.

Then there was that dark night
when I was dragged away,
My hair gripped, my dignity pulled
As my body cleansed your castle floor,
Purifying the pillars you so thoughtlessly gambled away.
I was fire on that day too- a fire blazing for justice.
You- with your excuse called righteousness
And a blind kingdom to support your way,
Painted your name in the history of mankind

As someone forever defeated on that day.

I remember surrendering to my faith that night,
Or maybe I surrendered to my courage and my soul,
For not an eyelid did flicker,
Nor a voice make way to my side,
As Humanity was disrobed.

I remembered focusing on a light
Waiting for it to be over,
My flames engulfed my heart
Swearing a vengeance of a lesson.

After a while, I open my eyes,
Silence all around me,
My Being intact,
The assembly aghast and
Ego lay at my feet
As I vowed to cut off its branches
in the final battle.

One by one, the path led the future of the throne to me,
My fire blazed through kingdom and people
In a lesson that was to rage on for ages.

And even on that last day,
When balance was restored,

I- was still Fire,
You- remained defeated as always.

13

Yours lovingly,
Draupadi

-Suranjali Seal

Hope

Dear Hope,

Be the wind
And seep through my feathered skin,
Lifting me up,
As I mend myself for tomorrow.
For if it wasn't for you,
We'd all be wingless birds,
Caged within ourselves,
Oblivious to the open skies.

-Suranjali Seal

Wish

Dear You,

May your tears always nourish the soil
that sprouts a better day.

-Suranjali Seal

A Teacher

I leave a little space in my heart,
To house your life and its story,
I help open the doors to rooms
that define your life,
Making a pathway out of that blessing,
For your walk towards the rising sun.
I wear a cloak of invisibility
Amidst crowds that cheer you on,
As you reach the sun and dissolve in its light,
Shining through the skies of success.
And as I walk back down Memory Lane,
That hosts your house of growth,
I smile to myself knowing that
Somewhere in your heart,
I too have made my own home,
Where our footsteps are decorated
In frames along the corridors.

-Suranjali Seal

Coffee

Let me be your respite in those midnight dreams,
And a recurring aroma in your heart -
Let me be your cup of coffee.

-Suranjali Seal

Night Has Come Early

You were the Autumn leaf
That I had so carefully tucked into my book,
And just as casually you left rustling by,
And with you all those pages took.

The weary steps of that cold feeling,
Consuming places left to reignite,
Morning is long gone,
The fire exhausted
And Night has come early tonight.

-Suranjali Seal

You

*Your love pushes through me to my heart
like the Ocean pushes through gravel and sand,
Cleansing the Shores insecurities
every time that they embrace.*

*Your smile greets me
like Sunlight meets snow-tipped mountains on winter
mornings,
And with all the joys that you bring,
You melt my heart like Winter does for Spring.*

*You cause ripples in my heart of sand,
Lightening in my sunny days,
Waterfalls in my ocean life,
I guess Love does work in mysterious ways.*

*You are my favorite corner of the room,
The favorite time of my day,
My rum, my cream and honey,
The flavor in my cocktail of life.*

-Suranjali Seal

Courage

I love how you dance on thin ice
without the fear of it breaking
and having you fall through,
Being who you are and chasing your dream
With an immovable focus and intentions true.

So as long as you are honest with yourself, remember
this
every time your zeal becomes a second guess,
That courage, hard work, fear, failure and hope
will always be the ornaments that
embellish the shoulders of Success.

-Suranjali Seal

Beautiful

You are like a waterfall -
Uncontrollable
Rushing
Tumbling
Falling

but, beautiful.

-Suranjali Seal

Rainy Days

*There is something so eternal about rainy days
that reminds me of the number of chapters
that this "pale blue dot" which we call our home
has composed and continues to do so everyday.
Just like the rain washes away
the dregs of dust off of every
petal, leaf and stone,
We, our insignificance and pride
are washed away in the end
by Time.
Thunder, lightening, puddles and pools are
perhaps one of the only constants
that have watched over us as we
passed through time and space
in multiple civilizations.*

-Suranjali Seal

Through My Window

I sometimes ponder at the world that my my bedroom
window
periodically opens towards and closes from.
Today, it opened up to Night and her stardust skies
greeted me kindly.
The creatures of the night continue to talk.
The Wind carries their voices to my window.
The Moon presides over their meeting
and I lay on my bed, quietly listening.
Then comes the motorized roar of a vehicle from a
distance,
Ignorantly dispersing the echoes of the night
Which continue to navigate their way to my window.
They are saying something - this orchestra of nature-
Giving a tune to a conversation of grave importance.
I focus on this song and gradually,
All man-made things begin to disappear.
I find myself lastly on the milky way,
Appreciating just 'being',
These creatures of the night-

Are they talking about us?
Perhaps. Who knows?

25

-Suranjali Seal

Yours Truly

I rest on a tilted tripod,
Watching the sun sink into the sky,
My world is a world within a world,
It's wonderful!- this world that I call mine .
In vain I try to word the feelings
That I myself don't understand,
But, as the words go lost and found,
They unburden me of the mysteries of my heart,
For Poetry knows my feather cuts
And diamond dreams
And materializes my reveries,
A companion of much help
In my solitary adventures
Into Myself.

Yours truly,
A Poet

-Suranjali Seal